the bridge from day to night

DAVID ZIEROTH

the bridge from day to night

poems

HARBOUR
PUBLISHING

HARBOUR PUBLISHING CO. LTD.
P.O. Box 219, Madeira Park, BC, VON 2H0
www.harbourpublishing.com

Edited by Silas White
Cover photo of the Second Narrows Bridge by Margery Patrick Zieroth
Cover and text design by Shed Simas / Onça Design
Printed and bound in Canada
Printed on FSC-certified and 100% post-consumer fibre

Harbour Publishing acknowledges the support of the Canada Council
for the Arts, which last year invested $153 million to bring the arts to
Canadians throughout the country. We also gratefully acknowledge
financial support from the Government of Canada and from the Province
of British Columbia through the BC Arts Council and the Book Publishing
Tax Credit.

LIBRARY AND ARCHIVES CANADA CATALOGUING IN PUBLICATION
Zieroth, David, author
    The bridge from day to night / David Zieroth.
Poems.
Issued in print and electronic formats.
ISBN 978-1-55017-835-7 (softcover).--ISBN 978-1-55017-836-4 (HTML)
    I. Title.
PS8599.I47B75 2018   C811'.54   C2017-907499-7
                                              C2017-907500-4

for Evan, Liam, Robin

in memory of Bernice (1935 - 2017)

*Each day marks fresh hours of effort to keep
pure and clear the life story one has inherited
from yesterday.*
—James Hamilton-Paterson, *Griefwork*

contents

3

1

North Van morning

the ships glide
slowly under a red
apparatus lifting containers
from rusty decks
above the water, each crane
a Trojan Horse

the SeaBus - the *Otter*? -
passes under its regard
its power
to raise the materials
we desire passed on
to the men and women
who cross below, reading
or gazing into thoughts

on a routine morning
a siren cleaves through
to the edge
of consciousness, a crow
calling from the conifers
the tallest branches of
alders click in a code
no one gets anymore
although squirrels
scrambling through the vines
stop and listen

zero energy after work

I kick off my shoes, drop
papers wanting my hand
under direct light, throw my coat
fix my path on evening's couch: being
gravely horizontal, looking up
but glazed, watching
not the spider in the front door corner
but scenes repeating
words sudden and said

I drift and lift off and float down
my street, peer into windows still open
sun now beyond black mountains
no one drawing the drapes
still reliving the commute
arriving to grip amber glass
or finger white china, tap
on the chintz edge

when I roam too far, I cross above
the man who curls on the sidewalk
by the veggie restaurant, his head
a red toque, under piles of plaid blankets
yellow milk crate for his brown banana
air turning to steam above his face
a sunburnt whiteness, a witness
arresting above damp concrete
I dip down here
nudge his shoulder, touch his bearded cheek
tell him the angel of warmth
comes to bear him to a new hearth
to bathe him, feed him, but not
bind him to regular hours
not require of him to surrender his search
for butts and bottles nor even demand
he learn anew how to look
at our passing faces

maritime clouds

their steel bellies have brought
the warm air of the ocean
from some island we can smell
so that in the closed dark
of the night we push open
our windows and feel again
the elements of air and water
entering us, making us
ourselves under maritime
clouds, the rushing, pushing
mass that says no sun today

just that sweet moist air
and the calling of the crows
that have been greeting it
since light began, not long
ago, when we stood trembling
like good dogs at the start
of a hunt, we who are waiting
for a change, that turn of the
earth that is really a lurch
into pungent spring
coming on an offshore wind
to find us overdressed
in down, our throats white
from winter, our eyes
cold and inward

man at bus stop

...watches cars
wrinkled lanky folds
lean on advertising

for the uncommon convertible
his eyes narrow
he scuffs dirt

women rushed from home
kiss someone smaller
twist a skirt to face front

my own change ready
lining up
counting items on the ground
butts, bags, stones
part of a wing

Lucifer's kiss

I haven't been paying ample attention again
I have been walking as a cloud under clouds
I unwittingly gain on man and dog: we enter a narrow
passage, the man, heavy, holds keys and chain
and then, without seeing me, unlocks his truck door
unsnaps the cur who turns and growls

black dog – smooth hair, blunted tail, long legs –
turns to find me too close, gargles his canine venom
frightful brightness of yellow-white teeth leaps
from his muzzle, so I pull back, right arm rising up
beside my body the way stroke victims carry
that unbending appendage useless against attack

I shrink, though I'm sure this menace senses
I am not afraid of mutts, my arm jerks up
against my thorax, involuntarily protecting my core
the man turns, silver face hair carefully groomed
shouts, 'Lucifer!' and shakes his chain, while I huff
'good name for him!' – adrenaline in my voice

pushing me past – while he apologizes, 'his bark's
worse than his bite,' which is true, I admit, because
he *has* bitten me, though not with his jaws, he's driven
his snout against my hip, the weight of a nightstick
I feel it still, the force of that kiss, knowing I am lucky
his is not the devil's bite I first feared, like those

in other times when a bright blackness drew near
on animal feet, snarled and snapped, forced you
to choose how to act: withdraw and pray
or kick and yell, swear and run, strike back, curse
or acquiesce and fall under fangs, submit to fate
to get past, back at last into yourself without shame

coat hangers

triangular forms hold sweaters, shirts
I close the closet door
leave them to their work-dark
where some continue to play
a little music as I walk away

sometimes at the very back
behind the sports coat I cannot
bear either to pitch or wear
I see a wooden kind, from my father's time
when a dark suit would be held and held and held
and taken down once for merry
and once for dead
it makes no sound, stiff and thick
ungainly among the tingling
new thin wire wisps
eager to touch one another and set off
the tiniest spark of sound
multiplying

all hang and wait for a hand
to take, to use, to return them to their hooked
lives in the crowded fusty room
their burdens dropping straight down
all their conversations saying
new replaces old
old becomes odd
migrates to the back, unconsulted
about the jingling

on the usually overlooked

between sidewalk slabs a little dirt
collects, in the place where concrete
meets and allows itself to open
to the earth that falls in and the earth
that seeps up, sweeps in, takes up
residence, waiting for good seed
to arrive: a bird dropping twigs
or splatter, or a big-foot dog finally
shaking burrs from his coat
or from gusts of wind bursting

the grass in the crack is never quite
so green as its counterpart on the lawn
never so robust, seldom maturing
yet still it grows, it does not judge
nor does it descend into self-pity
it sees itself as the hardier
withstanding boots and sandals
children with their digging fingers
each small tuft of green isolated and
individual, drawing the child's attention

either one or one of the multitude
what matters more is how each differs
in being trod upon, though what springs back
for air and sun is the same need
for light and the caprice of rainfall

machine

not just grain elevators on the harbour
- huge blocks upright with fans big as houses
starting weekday mornings, a synthetic screech
sending noise into upslope streets -

but every neighbour building or rebuilding
with hammer, crowbar, oath, as sudden
toothed blade bites board and snaps
up its end with the finality of a jaw

and a hungry young crow complains
calling, calling, gets to gargle on
remains of mouse stuck down its red maw
lust sated and turned again to hoarse cawing

who has not spoken about machines
even in his smallest voice half-aware
how sound is building until soon he roars
without knowing (why) he is shouting?

but now Sunday-still six a.m., soft air comes down
from mountains, gulls are elsewhere
squawking on thermals, breeze brings
only one many-blocks-away dog baying

and even he stops, must cock his ear
to hear small birds again, chickadees formerly
lost to the machine, especially that bridge
of car, shunting train, semi truck, and diesel's

blaring acceleration through amber light
air-filling and -killing blasts from rear
pipes, end products of honks and heat
- all faint at last, quiet on this front

till a squirrel's sudden skid by my lawn chair
makes me shout out loud lump of sounds
– then from his safe tree accuses me of crimes
equal to the machine, accursed

noisome interferer of the natural path

man on the SeaBus reading

ignoring red harbour cranes outside
concentrating on yellowing paperback
he's younger than I, yet in his mouth
turned up to focus on sentences, in his
modern click-pencil, I see myself
underlining old pages, holding gingerly
bent edges, not one to break a back
I glance at the title, dismiss it, return to
his face, his single-mindedness intense
not distracted by my intent looking

we disembark and stride together
for a while, side by side, silent as friends
who have no need for speaking, and then
the crowd heaves, he is lost, I am contained
among shoulders not bumping, shrunken space
skilfully manoeuvred up escalators with
phones, purses, packs, jewels in ears
and lips and noses, rows of noses, coughs
and coffee cups, shiny hair and hubbub
some to trains, some to city streets

that night I find my own copy
spine cracked, nearing end of usefulness
scan the sentences once meaningful
those I underlined or ticked, ideas of time
that now seem banal – and thus mysterious:
who was I to have thought like this? –
how I have continued to adjust
and what is here has not – and again
I return to that stranger, wonder how far
he has to travel, by what train or bus
on foot, among crowds, alone, jostled, and
if he might reach among the muddles

a clearing, brought there
by words, the apprehension
announced by his sudden sigh
recognizing a true place .

this Sunday morning

...all is quiet except for
the van that runs through
the streets to save an old man
or a drunk when the bells
from the mission church ring out
and tell us to grow into stillness
which the birds, who have been awake now
for many hours, can fill with their songs
especially the rufous-sided towhee
who says from the tree near me
'accuse me, accuse me' –

of what I can't think, his life
the unfailing movement from tree
to feeder, the one the old woman
has put out so she can see
the new birds and the old
count her favourites
and increase her life list
by yet another migrant passing through
the most beautiful lazuli bunting
that cannot be mistaken for
a bluebird, either eastern
or western, but is only
himself although we never hear him
enough, his song small in the clamour

the way the piercing one note
from the yellow-shafted flicker
stitches up one side of the ravine to the other
or the rasp of the young crow
as the adults stuff down yet
more junk into his red gullet
not much different from that
of the puking drunk now
in the back of the cruiser
trying to get to the window

which won't open
his own hand smelling as it comes up
to hold back in his mouth
what last night it took pleasure
in putting there

I sit here with my head turned
to the window, to catch the bells
far enough away that some Sundays
the wind takes their delicate reminder
elsewhere, falling on a street
empty of cars where only a dog
crosses at an angle, his tongue
hanging down and his mouth
sweet from the hunt

lilacs

if only the distance between desires
and me were wider than the walkway's
invitation to stroll among new lilacs
the short time they live with us, soon
rust brown, fragrant only days –
and so pervasive, persuasive the wanting
that overtakes me as I sling my body
along, inviting me to reconceive of
various places it might belong

midway in their transient time
lilacs tease with scent, remind me
I am an earth-thing: fully here
even when travelling toward not-to-be
with edges and urges best left
on beaches, where salt and wind
draw from my skin its remembering
and failures to grasp what comes
when guts will shrivel and
cease – yet I might also
jump to counter-scenes that
revive: how to live with that woman...
live like that man... laugh like
their child, leap like her dog...

eyeful

harbour overflows with steel
each ship such a size
my eye disbelieves their floating
from where I walk
among trees, earth's best
yet modest show, and hear
up ahead in aspens
a gallery of remarks
from starlings, nervous talk
some days I understand

almost, and pondering
the notes to gather in their tune
I forget how high
they perch, and walk beneath
step on white guano
glowing, one shape an Africa
wet on wet earth, post-fuel
expulsions scribbled below
while high comments continue
on harbour hulks, on why
hunched crow at branch four
refuses to leave, how the man
looks up, ducks, dodging
slippery reconnection

back to a jagged pebble
kicked into blackberry bramble
without knowing
what the foot has done, hearing
only a small atonality in shoe-squeak
on its leap forward

...a child stops on the street and tries to pry
from concrete the stuck-on part of a wing
some hatchling that grew big but could not
fly and was crushed, body so scant it
vanished under rain and beaks of crows

only ribs of desiccated primaries remain –
and these he wants to lift up, but his mother
scolds him, laughing, nonplussed he has
yet to learn what cannot be safely touched
and this stir returns to the boy later

when he has sons of his own, sees so often
hazards of the day, learns not to fear them
entirely and thus is pierced hearing his
mother's mirth, she among the long dead
her shining hair once constant, comforting

gone, and he recalls a purple shadow
fleeting through that breath: his father
peered down as if he, too, could toy with
an emptiness that yet wanted holding
as it called out for a child's moist hand

wind

...moves the slender leaves of the yellow iris
and they turn rather than bend, stiff guards protecting
soft petals through their short preciousness
I have seen it tangle leaves from dissimilar plants
and both the shrub and the young tree have tossed
wanting to be free, some twist of disgust touching
each the same way – and fair enough, I say
I don't ever imagine I'd expect to be held
or to hold for more than that brief afternoon
we wanted to be released not from each other
so much as from ourselves: we were green and
growing up, reaching for sun, wind
made us supple, cooled us down, taught us to linger
and listen to the rattling leaves, dizziness
subsiding in us we noticed still hovered among
ever turning and reflecting prisms of green
and pale white, all eating at light with mouths
as our mouths had once touched each other
as we had said certain loving words and then
let them escape, grateful for the working wind

dream of song

I fail to finish my thesis, and my house
agonizes until I am accompanied by
two strangers who walk me away
from the piles of paper and its acid smell
man on the left, woman right

on the street, I am able to sing
songs spontaneous and melodious
about all that passes before us
a dog, his tail wagging rightly
turns a corner and flashes us
a look of fellow joyfulness
I sing about sandwich boards
advertisements, opticians, trash and
sirens, sunken old faces
a baby looking up from his pram
eager to see us before we proceed

though he seems not to see the two
who walk with me, perhaps because
I am the only one singing
even as I know they also can sing
but they are silent beside me
and slightly behind, both tall
and straight, and my power to sing
of every object we see or encounter
derives from their silence

only later at the beginning of the end
when I rise slowly into myself again
only then do I wonder why I never thought
to sing of *them*, and how I ache now, still
having missed that song – had I turned
to look into their high faces just once –
and how I missed as well their very voices
so overjoyed was I by their voice in me

the bridge from day to night

driving back on the Second Narrows
I see the mountains of North Van
rise higher than I imagine
they can, they keep going
up and up, and from the apex
of the bridge with traffic flying
I look directly into
their deepest clefts:
a bear drifts on the trails
and a hiker half falls down
the slope, one arm out
for a sapling to swing around

it's home (box in a box)
that will save me (if not him)
yet I sometimes can't decide
should I go up the Cut
or turn on Main, the only options
I see right now, though late at night
when I give up the day
I dream the bear comes calling

2

first thought

of all my thoughts, one thought
is the first - it came to me
when I was a child and lives in me still
but which thought, and how
to find again one slim stick
amid the many limbs of the forest
verdant and grey, dry and budding
cunningly intertwined, stuck and
holding against night and wind and
violent squabbling in the air

each day the thoughts erect a wall
and tell me not to look
back into the tangled garden
where someone like me
once lived, it was me, yes, me
though I would have placed the chairs
differently, not so near the pond and
so many cups of suddenly spilled tea
can only mean the guests have gone

the kick

only person alive who knows this story
is me, how I was nagging my mother, my
little boy's voice growing bolder as she bent
over the counter pushing out cinnamon rolls
how she didn't mind my disrespect
really, but my father in the living room
could no longer bear my tone, and he came
through the doorway toward us holding
his newspaper and shouted at me to stop
his pitch loud, louder than mine
and I could tell his temper
could not be contained, when he
shot out his right foot to kick me

but I was agile, leapt away, his
wool socks slipped, he lost
footing, and with one leg up
slid down to the floor while I fled
and in my flight I heard my mother
laugh, the fall of authority always funny
although I did not think that then

frightened he'd find my bedroom
closet where I hid, silent and
fingering squares of fabric my mother
would stitch into a patchwork pillow
I wished had curved under my father's
rump when he crashed, in a rage
that might not be softened in time

which allows imagination to mislead
memory, although not in all cases
for that swift current of air I felt
as my father's foot almost reached me
reaches me still, and it cannot be changed

the scene begins

...with people dispersing
in an open dance into which gallops
a chestnut horse huge with malice
flashing his eye, head tossing

two women the last to leave
have just fled when the animal
charges and only feet from me
makes an instantaneous, sparkling
molecular change into a ballet dancer
who skids up and speaks
her voice never heard before, so coarse
and worsened by the way she says
first 'follow the women'
then 'kill or be killed'

I run, and descending
from that schoolyard light
make my mistake: instead of
continuing on, I hurdle the fence
a picket of green and grey slats
each point softly weathered
an easy leap, then a dodge
into an alcove, hear hooves
on slate, snorting breath close

- and awake again out of
what I live and watch at night
this time an absurd picturing
a twofold message
someone might understand
or make something of
that might be right

but the jumping? – the boy in me
lives! the set stays well lit
my bounding over the fence fuelled
by a momentary grace in short pants
left runner unlaced

waiting for the wishbone

...to dry (several fingers vying for
tugs on the bird's
small fork) and me the youngest
too young to wish to elude
the trait found in uncles
who drank alone, no point
naming one dead before I was born

wish for summer sun
on heads, hands brown
bread from the oven
chicken, cinnamon buns
silence at the table for grace
then jabber, and after, men at ease
with toothpicks, cups of tea
before putting on caps
crossing back into sun

beams on the windowsill
suck up bone's springiness
and none of us thinking
how the days pass –
perhaps my father, who rarely
pulled, wished somehow
his brother could return –
as a kid this trick seemed
entirely possible
though already I felt
the selves of myself
pulled into other than
my meant-to-be

then the v-twig bends – breaks! –
releases winner's hurrah
above loser's harrumph –
me already pestering Mum
to still a living wishbone

with a fresh farmyard kill –
oh, years before compassion
enters, and even so
a farmer's child seldom weeps
for a pullet unless he sees
and names the smallest chick
and watches it grow

until he grasps how down
becomes bedraggled feathers
scales, a reptilian eye, beak
ready to peck anyone nearby
how pretty goes gross, how
a father and mother get tough

a king's ransom

when my teacher grew large with child
the fathers gathered, those not crushed
by a hardship of hail or drought
or freak flood, and determined that a man
would replace her (though males were rare –
straining, sweating elsewhere), one who
would take command and teach grades
one to eight whatever it was that brains
in far-off offices had established children
must grasp and take into their mass before
trading in books and desks for lives

the fathers settled on a young man not ready
for the world, and one day he talked to us
– we in rows, open as mouths, almost
eager, even older boys behind me –
and said something wrong: that 'priceless'
meant 'worthless,' and I began to argue
quoting my reading about a king's ransom
in a story I'd found in our library
smaller than the stinky cloakroom where
we hung our coats and toques jumbled
on hooks no one could claim as his own

I knew my father did not know how limited
a mentor had been brought before us, and
that evening as I sat at our table, I looked
at him again: he didn't notice me, busy
cutting potato pancakes, and I thought
perhaps he, too, failed to take in the word's
true meaning – but I soon corrected myself:
I had seen him reading, face alight, leaning
into the couch, winter storms heaving up
banks outside, and I supposed for now
his breadth of vocabulary surpassed mine

though mine was growing, pregnant with
distaste, and in time I gathered and hurled
words neither teacher nor parent
could doubt, my mouth wrought into
an *o* of outrage at what was amiss
not just at school, which I would leave
but in cities beyond, where I felt
next lessons hammer on my skin
every stage a spell of aching, and how
long – endlessly long yet almost missed –
before I grasped at last the matter most
precious between us: that we were alike
in our bodies, our girths and ears, our way
of walking, of holding back, his particulars
bequeathed, manifested, let loose in me

my father's talking to me

...volubly, pointing out below
the valley of small lakes gleaming up
where we're ledge-perched, the wind
inside our jackets, pulling our pockets
before he begins down the trail
into the bottomland, the shining lakes
waiting, to plant some new seed
of blue mirror sheen inside himself
we stop, he talks, and the stream of air
takes the words –

how the timbre of his voice
finds us equals today
and he can scrutinize terrain
as if I were his hunting partner
who knows the paths of animals
their spoor and signs few can read

but I've worn the wrong clothes
from the wrong era and cannot descend
into the valley of the many lakes
their fertile mud, the ducks
and deer, the tang of new willows

I take shelter by a leafless tree
he'll return to tell me
of his last steps into the moist
perpetual spring and summer
lean toward me and shout
against the gale force here, his mouth
near my ear, my head bent to hear him
glad to draw this close
to smell not his old-man
scent but the lily pollen
apple blossom, tiniest hint
of earth set to yield

a fox disguised

Do you know that foxes
believe in nothing
but themselves - everything
is a fox disguised...
—Alden Nowlan, 'Country Full of Christmas'

we have returned from the forest
to a large log house that old trees
surround still, and here we will
sleep in the many rooms, the many
of us, an older brother amongst us
and most already abed when I hear
a knocking on the second door
the one with the glass panel
through which I look and see the fox

but hadn't the fox been killed
earlier and weren't we the killers
hunting in that wide forest? truly
I cannot recall, but I know
the fox, once dead, now lives
and I call to my brother who leaps
from his bed and orders fortifications
to the house, then commands

that I must be the one
who opens the first door, to step out
and face the fox - and when I do
I discover there, waiting, lying long
and tawny, a deer! and with him
a doe and yearling, and now the stag
speaks to us, though no words
come through the air, speaking
in a new way, impossible
not to hear him, and he says
he has come for our protection
now it is hunting season

42

and as this stag walks toward me
through the light from the house
I see the shadow he casts
and his pointed ears and nose
are those of the fox
dark as the trees that release
dreams tossed up in rooms
of polished golden logs

Waldersee Church

I was a boy who sought and found
an oriole shadow falling from wind
past poplars onto our high house wall
and hearing his song, I leapt from
where I was lolling on the grass as
his sound swept along and kept me sweet

till an old woman died, a grandmother
last seen lying abed, air immovable
around her, sons back by the door
my own mother pale with grief
that her mother never did receive
the one flowered dress she desired
which my grandfather would not buy
his tight-fisted fear of not having dollars
deep inside the pockets he soon took
earthward, his stick left behind

and with that I had crossed a demarcation
understood death meant my mother's
dying, and I knew how I would fail
if she were not available for my ease
each day, and so I sat in that church
and wailed even louder than she
because I did not know of her relief
that the old woman had slipped past pain
uplifted somehow above the altar and
statue of Jesus, also immovable
in red robes, starred palms out

I brought from that forming hour a
precise smell of foliage: funeral wreaths
bore an acid scent (as if decay had
begun - and it had begun, I had to admit
its idea rooted in me did not die), whiff
I catch walking on November leaves
roused by a sun-borne breeze

Abbott and Costello go to the moon

I am less than ten
when they take that trip
I sit in the hall in the centre of town
not far from the windbreak
that holds back space
while here the light shoots out
and shines over those who begged
big coins from moms
and who sit now on hard seats
clutching tickets Eva gave
at the door, George climbing to the booth
and planning magic

two men toss tools
fall down and trip
building a rocket
up through their roof

my brother says 'stop wiggling'
his face still calm
I begin to hope heat from the bulb
will eat the pictures
these fools have learned
nothing from their mothers
their fathers too busy
to make the rocket work
unable to suggest
a second dream

perhaps George in his high office
has extra powers
he can send these fools so they might see

the folly of always falling down
and tripping up
and staying stuck
with one other

perhaps my brother
will tell me how to see their failure
as the pay at the end of the day
but I can no more ask him
than I can raise my hand
in this cave and stop
that light telling a story, and so
I bolt from my chair
down the row and out the door
past Eva, struck by my face
my mouth

I leave the light
and set my eyes on the plain
beyond the trees, what little
I can see in the moonlight
its emptiness only
what I put there

hallucinatory light

square of light, a barn window grimy and passed by
daily, hundreds of days, more than thousands, a beam
to throw at clouded pale nights, to illuminate
white radiant flakes falling so slowly I see
how each glows, is made to glow, by passing through
the animal shelter's muted brightness

one bulb above the round backs of cows, saddle
backs of workhorses always calm yet accustomed to
colossal acts of power, pulling the stone boat
while dreaming (it seems), even as rocks thrown in
threaten the boards onto which they fall

these large animals bathe in dimness, blurring
a bit, losing sureness found by outside sun in
pasture clarity, all of us rooted by light, exact
so strong no one could go wrong understanding
the place of... *things* – but in a barn at night
winter all around, the cold seeping up through
the floor, through walls, how good then to stand
with the beasts, soak them up by smell, remember
they live and die more easily than us
a last agony of bullet-in-the-head – and now
their unknowing sends off sound:
a lowing of steady godlike giving

after supper

...my mother returns when I'm washing up
doesn't inquire if I'm buying a machine –
irrelevant, from after her time – but asks
why I haven't yet learned to hold my words

she was in the wine store today when I lifted
up a Sangiovese and spoke to a stranger hunting
in our Italian aisle for another brand to add to
the two he'd rested in his black basket

she asks what I sensed in him was amenable
to random suggestion – 'try it, you'll like it' –
his lips quick to twist and reply, 'I already have'
she who foresaw his scorn more clearly than I

so I take note of her counsel for guardedness
and when she whisks away, I hardly know
she's been by except the plug's pulled
sink's swished clean, ready for tomorrow

and what remains? – her hands, fingers bent
and supple from dishes, washtubs, plucking
chickens, dipping them (dead, headless)
repeatedly in buckets of boiling water, then

singeing off pinfeathers with a red sheaf of
burning paper thrust up, flame sweeping
across flesh – and such hands unprotected in
hard acts never hardened their touch on me

a closer look

I step off the train into night's
ice crystal cave, underdressed
again, the cold here more northern
than in the city I have left behind
for now, where ideas
from lecture halls heat our streets

my mother is thinner, wool
coat falling mid-calf, fur hat
semi-Russian - and my father:
flaps of winter cap pulled down
over big ears, talking across
'58 green Impala - I hold back
unseen by them, wanting to see
how they look at one another

then I'm inside a café
I have entered whistling, farmers
in their Saturday night booths
looking up at my sound
I see my father eating soup
and slide in beside him - Mum?
'you just missed her, she caught
the train, she's gone to France'

touring sedimentary formations
famous in sunny Provence?
he orders soup for me, pulls a stone
from his pocket, places it
on the varnished tabletop: 'she wanted
to give you this,' and I pick up
a grey, distorted egg-chunk
from any gravelled road
anywhere on her earth

how much I am missing!
I imagine my mother with
a secret passion she acts on
I near the bottom of my bowl
and wonder: am I gemstone or lump?
I turn to my father: so he, too, doesn't
escape my present knowing
I take a closer look, to admire
the best found there, his long life
and kindness for an uppity son

the first time

I bend forward in a friend's house
to feel my knee-level grandson's
forehead on my lips, and I hope
he never remembers the first time
I kissed him - yes, let him think
my affection and the blessing of
this commonplace dropping off
began long ago in an age before
he knew its name now he's
grown past *car* and *owl* and *cookie*
and knows where to point:
up to jars of countertop treasures

and yes, he turned away from me
already busy watching the antics of
other children bouncing much
faster than any adult here, we
who admit sometimes to ignoring
the chatterers who must tell
their discoveries, that naptime
has changed from this to that
or perhaps that to this, we
missed it, those of us hip-holding
a baby while stirring and fetching
toys and relocating the cookies

- and now I recall my mother's
cinnamon buns, a morning's
production pushing out the elastic
dough that wanted to spring back
into a lump, anointing
the slab with butter, sprinkling
brown sugar so it glistened wet

then the dusting of spice before
rolling out a log she cut and slid
onto a greased sheet and into
the oven, but not before pinching off
a piece of raw sweetness for me

neighing, too

as one ages, the temptation
to overact increases
not from any *who cares?*
but rather *perhaps I'd better*
put my fingers in my mouth
stretch lips into a rectangle
to cause this tired grandson to smile
at my horse's tongue grossly pink
reaching through a farm fence
to rip up ripe, forbidden alfalfa

3

cure for colic

the baby will not be calmed until his father
needing to remind himself, opens a window
trees fling rain onto one another even while
the child hurls arms, arching spine so his mouth
falls open to reveal tongue quivering below eyes
shut but not so tight as to stop tears, surging
evidence of his pain and infant rage

suddenly he stops when new air drops on his
fontanelle, red from exertion, cool hand
of a natural, everyday god blessing him
an invitation to re-embrace what's wondrous
always waiting and from which we are made
raw, chirpy, damp, brisk and trilling yet ancient
describes splashes of feeling between father and son

outside: acoustically rich, beyond too familiar roars
of furnace and fridge, kisses and coos of mothers
tight handling of men holding him in elbow's crook
to face outwards near plink of dripping rain
till next he is carried to that outdoor sound
brought in to the tub, to distract, lull, enchant
and also teach him how to bathe in world-song

sleepwalking

I arose from my bed
walked out of my room, a boy
who found his way to the kitchen
pulled back a wooden chair
to climb on the table
where the previous evening
he'd sat with his family eating
pancakes, which perfected
in him the trick of walking
while asleep, softly
stepping past logic toward
the edge of the oilcloth
worn white from use and wiping

his mother standing below him now
arms upraised, hair dishevelled from
night, her face wearing that
old worry, always what if
she hadn't been there, and future
fears, for what of cars and
girls and finding somewhere
safer than this nighttime ledge

and the boy came awake to the thought
of the horses capable of standing
while sleeping, huge nodding heads
not bearing them to the ground –
he'd seen them lying flat
though rarely, and once one
stretched out and never did rise
to shudder off dust –
and day awareness came to him
in his desire to keep wakeful
somehow, even if his mother's arms
were welcome, and he did not mind
when she carried him back
to his still-warm bed, that space

sometimes like the one I inhabit now
in my daily to and fro
and out of which I wonder
when I might awaken

moon

man walks tonight with moonlight
on his left shoulder, a pale badge
on his winter wool coat, shield
for deflecting any icy wind toward
shrubs about to shiver

on an uphill street
his neighbours clicked off, cozy
and in dreams, alone whatever else
may occupy their beds
he roams on and stops under silent
shedding trees that have rooted
and then rotted, no longer
touched by children

moon sends him back to find
the two-year-old peering up
spying the changing white shape
sky-hanging, magnetized by magic
that it dangles always for him
wavers there now, close enough
he must once have touched it

at his door with the squeak
the tumblers in the deadbolt
align, the placement of adult shoes
outside, one pair tipped, two aright
then opening into a dark hall
transom blooming with silver

Pacific time

I have no one
who lives later
I can't phone
at midnight
out to the ocean where
she'd be fresh
willing to take my call
on her yacht
in the storm that breaks up
our telephone waves
and back east, prairie and
forest people curl asleep
in quilts, snow hushing past
while the night lights
blaze and tell them
it's time for the dream

I put down the phone
and wait and wait, wait
for the night to flow
and for the light to bring
active life to my window
a dove made from cloud
and the scent of juniper
turning round and round
on my ledge, a mate
already winging down

the photographer

...at the edge of this group of alert men
- all men - in the concentration camp, all
wearing ties because it's Christmas Eve
(so says a propped sign with Gothic letters)
German emigrants collected
by the *War Measures Act* in 1915
O, Canada! you do not know
the silences you have bequeathed unto
generations because no man here could breathe
knowing the outgoing air would shatter
all beliefs with the violence of its yell

sitting two men away from my grandfather
at the end of the row where he's just
nipped in, the photographer is pert, peering
into his own camera set up to take in
these lines of prisoners, their tinsel tree
the bent mattresses in the bleachers
of the fairgrounds where they sleep
some leaving behind a corpse
swinging, which internees see first
come morning and cold and gruel from
other-accented guards with Ross rifles
and long-reaching bayonets

my grandfather sits here, shocked rigid
what of his wife on her own, on the hard farm
and with children? I see his panic
the mark of betrayal on his face
that he was invited (like many)
to occupy the West, that he left
his ancestral home not knowing
the drift of history would ensnarl him
and, today, he's determined to show
that whatever the camera captures
it is not humiliation swelling within

large, brown gelding

...serves by pulling and stopping, then
pulling again, hard, side by side with
the black mare, head down, braced to haul
a load of stones – I remember mostly stones
and hot hairy rumps, hiss of their tails
against cruel flies, large liquid eyes
a child dives into and imagines himself
some other being, greater than mere boy
until one day the gelding's replaced: a mule
grey-wizened in harness, glory-lacking
but not dead – I rail at my mother: why
was I not told, why did I not deserve
to know? she says little, says my father
will have the answer – and so he enters
our presence striding, cracked leather boots
and cracked leather face like that of
a Balkan partisan who fights in winter
and has no patience for chatting
about natural dying that any worthy son
would absorb or toss behind him
he says 'appointments' and explains
no further, lets words fade, shorthand
he expects me to grasp, and I see now
he is old, as I am also old and must save
my rage for matters other than death
and in what is not said I hear where next
I must learn to live – and before I turn
to own my adult ache, I think of the gelding
wanting no more than his burden
of inevitability, and I promise to hold to
the memory of his strength, his last
groan of power spent departing, leaning
under a heavy sun, the very one
making my father fret, his worn boots
scuffing dirt, raising a snowy dust

grief

massive waves of it await us
(or the dread has already happened)
muscles in our organs
draw away from contact with skin
and contract so blood drains
out of toes and fingers foreign
in the face of sorrow, so contorting
its strength, tasted by all
each swallow a separate flame

details and particulars: So-and-so
falls ill on Wednesday and by Sunday
a coma envelops him in a cloud
of unknowing, and those dear
want one more word, a blessing
crazy talk, a drugged rant
will suffice: to hear
his voice once more

in after-days when love
requires documents and fire
to help the living
part with dregs of the dead, when woe
wells up to saturate, even then
someone wonders how to grasp
the space a person emptied
what words to manifest aftermath
of daily life, itself so necessary
our wonderer worries that nothing
better might ever be

last thoughts of the suicide

the last thought of the suicide was not of us
or of the rose that huddles on his balcony
where winter has left finger-cold snow
on morning's grey rail, setting colour
to shimmer so the red blooms anew

the living wish his death not to descend
and remind them how easily the insufficiency
of the world can be stormed, breached
how the logical end is death: thus to stop
present pain and future's sorrow at once

was it dignity he felt when the room
faded off, blocked by some slow process
that crept up his length and made him cold?
we do not want him thinking of the chaos
he bequeathed, toothpaste splatters, takeout

cartons, unforgivable shapes of his shoes
a team can be hired to wipe him out, leave
his home off-white, refreshed by labour
by windows open to street life where snow
announces both warning and brightening

we call to him now as we never called
before, cursing him for pointing out none of us
was ample bulwark against his own worst
and final thinking, which was not of our sadness
nor of the way a rose can bloom in winter

murder

it's night, a bedroom window open
so a woman pulled from sleep hears
'you are dead, you are so fucking dead'
and then a bottle smashes

guys shout, and a neighbour yells
'what's going on?' and the woman
remembers how once she coveted
that ground floor apartment

then someone running
and sudden outrage: 'he stabbed him
he stabbed him!' and cops
fast to arrive turn out the dog

in the movie version we'd cut
to the body, graze it lovingly
with our fuzzy lens or zoom in
for a final convulsion paramedics recognize

the hospital up the street
too far away – here they see him leaving
and stuff his wounds anyway, not the first time
for either, but still they stagger: a body

drained by pain, beyond writhing
ascending past iron balconies
where urban dwellers have turned
back to their clocks and shelves

shocked that here are things unchanged
when down on their common patio
'a severely injured male' stained first
the concrete and then the gravel

while that other runs and runs still
his knife folded away into himself
not in hand, his blood firing
again every time he remembers

the sudden swing of his arm

dream after euthanasia

driving my old car
in the backseat, keeshond cross
as she was the day the vet came:
hip so lumpy she leans
on the wall for balance

I'm opening the hood of the car
and sparked by nearby woods, she
lifts her head and leaps out
her animal engine running
stretches low to the ground

I yell her name, afraid to lose her, give chase
but she's vanished among trees
all standing identically and saying nothing

I come upon two figures bent toward
a dog between them, their pet now
- though more Rottweiler
than expected - they call her Springer

back at the car, I discover that it, too
has changed, starts easily
and I drive off, remembering

after the vet gently said *now*
after drugs entered via a back-leg vein
how the fur on her head
stayed soft

mice

two grey corpses on wet soil
heads a third of their mass
tiny feet up in supplication
to Tom-Tom, black cat who
caught and left them uneaten
Purina tastier than mouse

I hated nightly scuttling
yet as I walk past these two
in the already greening garden
a little shudder awakens my
pathos for their smallness
how they must often be least
among others, ears so big
of no use now, pressing dirt

were they related? brothers?
or a pair ready to mate near
neighbour's compost where
black fate dropped on them
fangs sudden and merciless
and bite after bite brought
squeals and then stillness
unseen in life of any size

Meg, Erik and the next life

when Meg asked Erik what animal
he wanted to be in his next life, he said
he hadn't learned enough in this one
and he had to come back as a human

it was a family question Meg asked
posed for their mother as she lay dying
'a river otter' was her reply, visualizing it
an immediate aid to her diving away

telling me this story made Meg smile
her cheeks growing more apple-like
though her brother's imminent death
was now the new normal, so close to her

every day an accounting of the changes
Erik himself watching when he could
and finding there new thoughts
we came to understand as our own

I want God

...or gods, Big or small, One
or all, more than me
to lean upon, give solace
(if not an entire guarantee)
let the flow of feeling
arise elsewhere and
I promise to erect homage
daily, in my garden
You nudge me at times, truly
You do, and then You vanish
taking even hope so that
the mildest insight must
suffice, its intimation of immortality
more kind than accurate

I know even talking this way
suggests why You left
asking why I couldn't surrender
what it was I thought
I would lose, and
why I didn't think more of the gain
(if not the entire guarantee)

a place in the Rockies

...my friend speaks of
as his choice of where to die:
high in a mountain glade
he would reach by leaning into
the slope, pushing step after step
up, wind after his very breath
stealing it from his mouth
so he yawns and stops to grab
at seed heads along the trail
crushing, then sniffing
their fragrance – and is it this scent
that brings him back to us
an earth-borne weed that tells him
he is leaving us behind, and then
for a moment does he turn back
weeping? – or has he already passed
beyond bonds others have
cast upon him, knowing
that open sky awaits his final
desire, when he will throw
his focused and tired totality
upon the serrated horizon before
lying down on pointed white stones
so that later, after the plucking
of ravens and the tearing
force of bears, one white thigh bone
remains ungnawed and matches
snow that covers it even in
spring when chinook winds
bring a jewelled downpour, enough
to loosen the skull from mud
and set it rolling again until
it stalls, sleeping in tall grass
at the base of a pine where a fox
sticks his snout through an eyehole

smelling mice and finding instead
the idea of mice, so startling here
in wilds men pass through
dreaming of an elsewhere

the shame of death:

that we are now
shining as thought
and so light from
incarnating as if
nothing else is

and that *even so*
we suffer death

I rise
but not so far, not so far
to outfly dying
a failure for a while
until I think
what is coming must be
as strong as I
in the struggle

only the blue spruce
at my window
will see how we grapple

no one will bear witness
or report back
how I might twist
and yearn to speak
before closed down at last

for such a tale
would only extend
to all who hear it
a quaver that heralds
the decomposition like-kind
must turn away from

the gradual desiccation of the dying

he came out of the not yet
bulldozed wild place
twitched in the sun
the repulsive rodent

because he was crazed by poison
he chose our street
for the scene of his dying
the flies first to arrive

then cars and the crushing began
although the tail remained robust
as did the yellow teeth:
a science experiment in metamorphosis

how long will his air overpower
the fragrant blossoms of the chestnut
above, as if he intended
to serve us his worst at the end

no one dares scoop or
fling the local back to his trees
each of us needs distance from
what produces puke before compassion

still later I kick his flattened corpse
to the gutter, and it skids on concrete
a broken valise, weightless
on this segment of the journey

the intolerable now

several hundred thousand moments
fall into me
and take up shape and look out and ask
'what now?'

what I am
makes minutes come and go
and do I believe
they do best
when they evanesce?

I am floating
not above but in
a timelessness
and I cannot be reached

not now
in the intolerable now

medical event

he stood up, said he felt
light-headed, sat down
turned green, then
grey – and collapsed
consciousness gone
instant cadaver
slumped in a chair

others knew what to do:
one fished for his tongue
another called 911
someone pulled him
onto the floor, bent over
pressed mouth on mouth
while I, down on my knees
held his bony hand, gibbering

one minute passed, a second
then his tongue flopped out
a welcome pink and
thick night animal
and he half-opened his eyes
colour flowing under his skin

an allergic reaction to wine
all tests at Emergency passed
though in his swift shift from vigour
to ashen stillness on the floor
I believed him dead

none of us knowing where
he had gone, not even he
when he was no longer here
each of us stayed lost
for a while because of his violent
absence, and we went hunting for

what haunted us: the flickering
when we mumble out a name
over and over, wanting back
time not yet held by silence
across which no words reach

self-reliance in old age

in any age, what friends want for me
the poet returned to
his abandoned manuscripts
their clank and clutch enough
to rebelieve - let me be the air
that enters with the scalpel's thrust

let me *not* be alone
as the hours fall and fail
or rather let aloneness befriend
the boy in me whose eye
looks to the horizon
chaff in his hair, grain in his hand

let no fly of inconsequence
bother him, let his youth
brim and hold and stay steady
so one day he may relocate
the naysaying self safely
there, to be remade

in the years that follow
and lead to peace, some say, which some say
cannot be found unless friends abound
even those who fall away
so many already dissolving
in words of their own

acknowledgments

Special thanks to those who read various versions: Robert Adams, gillian harding-russell, Lorna McCallum, Meg Stainsby, Richard Therrien, Russell Thornton.

Some of these poems have appeared in *The Fiddlehead*, BC *Studies*, *Literary Review of Canada*, *The Goose*.

An earlier version of the poem 'a fox disguised' appeared in *Seek It: Writers and Artists Do Sleep*, Red Claw Press, 2012.

An earlier version of the poem 'I want God' appeared in *The Poet's Quest for God: 21st Century Poems of Faith, Doubt and Wonder*, Eyewear Publishing, 2016.